Twenty to make

Necklaces

Stephanie Burnham

Search Press

First published in Great Britain 2008

Search Press Limited
Wellwood, North Farm Road,
Tunbridge Wells, Kent TN2 3DR

Text copyright © Stephanie Burnham 2008

Photographs by Debbie Patterson at
Search Press Studios

Photographs and design copyright
© Search Press Ltd 2008

ISBN-13: 978-1-84448-310-5

Suppliers

If you have difficulty in obtaining any of the
materials and equipment mentioned in this book,
then please visit the Search Press website for
details of suppliers: www.searchpress.com

Dedication
For Rosemary who always seems
to know when I have an available
'window' in which to fit new projects
– it's all your fault! Lots of love. X

Bead sizes
6mm = $\frac{1}{4}$in
8mm = $\frac{5}{16}$in

Contents

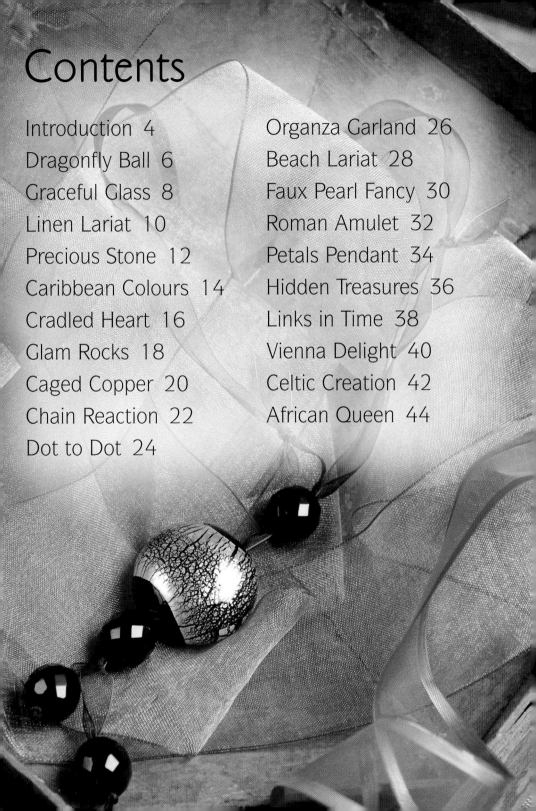

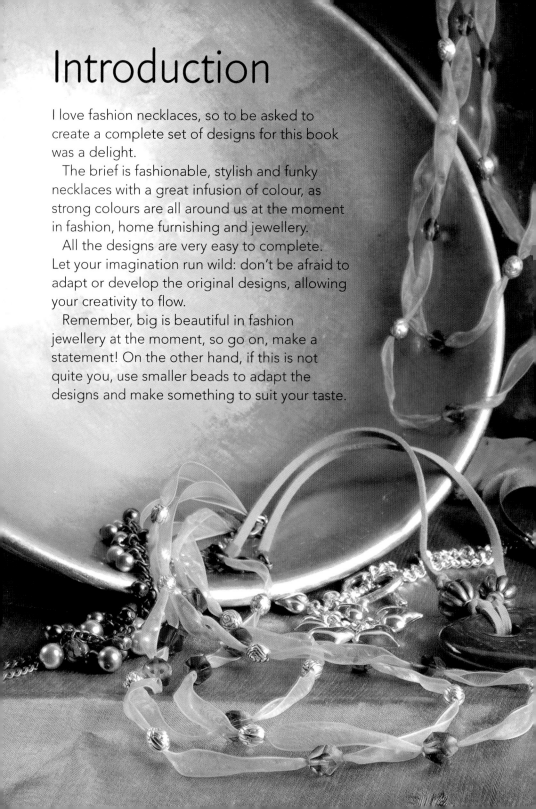

Introduction

I love fashion necklaces, so to be asked to create a complete set of designs for this book was a delight.

The brief is fashionable, stylish and funky necklaces with a great infusion of colour, as strong colours are all around us at the moment in fashion, home furnishing and jewellery.

All the designs are very easy to complete. Let your imagination run wild: don't be afraid to adapt or develop the original designs, allowing your creativity to flow.

Remember, big is beautiful in fashion jewellery at the moment, so go on, make a statement! On the other hand, if this is not quite you, use smaller beads to adapt the designs and make something to suit your taste.

Dragonfly Ball

Materials:

1 metre (39½in)
   craft chain

6 x dragonfly charms

Large toggle clasp

8 x jump rings

Tools:

Cutting pliers

Round-nosed pliers

Instructions:

1 Measure and cut a length of chain so that it fits around the neck and in addition to this, has a drop section long enough to hang the charms from.

2 Attach the loop part of the toggle to one end of the chain using a jump ring.

3 Using a jump ring, attach the T-bar end to the chain where you wish the chain to join at the front of the neck, allowing the section of chain at the end to fall down towards the chest.

4 Attach the charms using jump rings, starting at the base of the drop and working upwards so that the charms just about touch each other, thus avoiding any gaps in the design. Attach four to the drop and two to the section that goes round the neck.

Silver Hearts

Hearts in various sizes replace the dragonflies in this sumptuous silver version of the necklace.

Graceful Glass

Materials:

Glass pendant

50cm (19¾in) faux suede
ribbon in two colours

2 x flat leather crimps

2 x jump rings

Lobster clasp

Tools:

Flat-nosed pliers

Scissors

Instructions:

1 Cut both pieces of suede ribbon
to the required necklace length.

2 Pass both pieces through the
loop on the pendant.

3 Fix the flat leather crimps to both
ends of the necklace.

4 Attach a jump ring to one side of
the necklace and a jump ring and
the lobster clasp to the other.

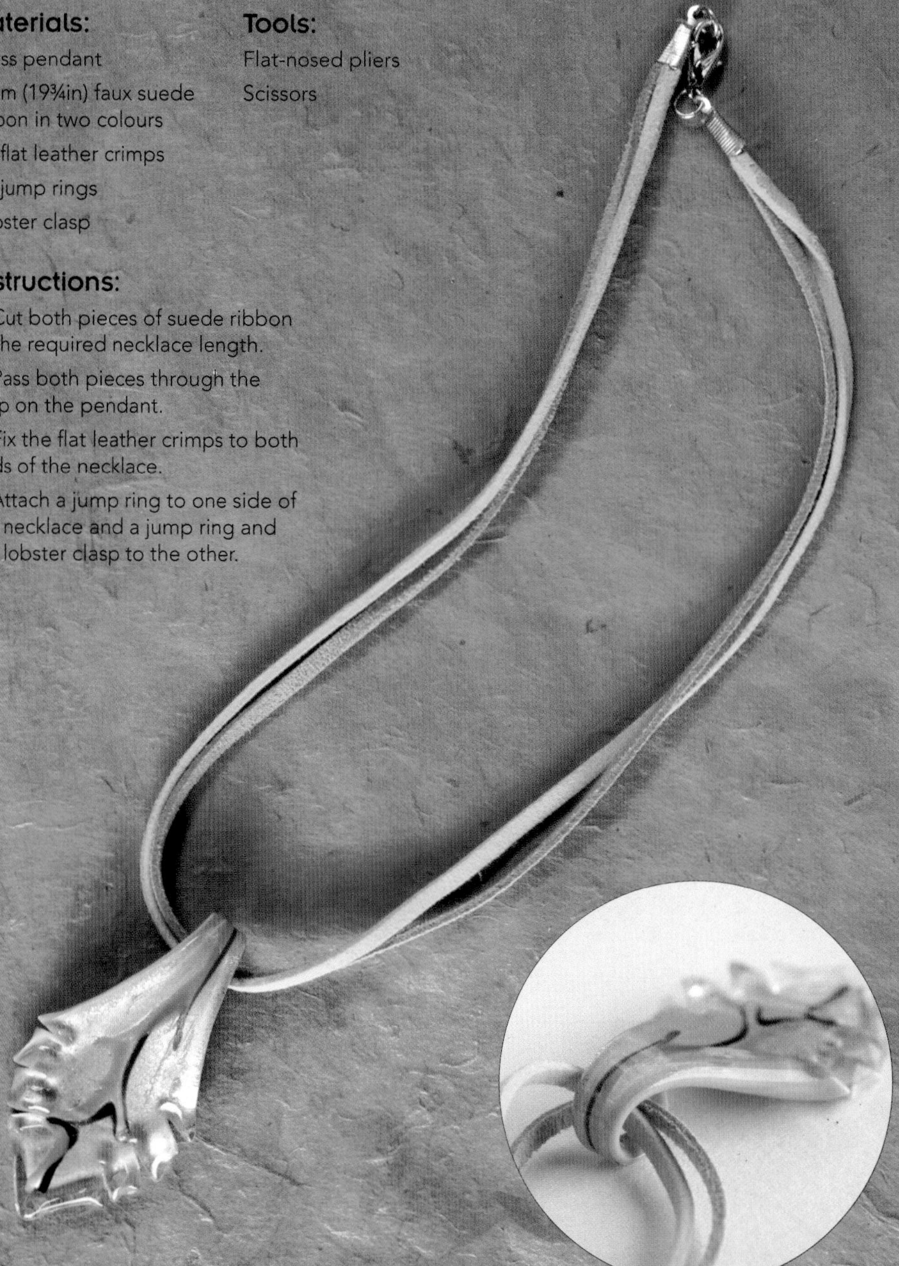

Gold Leaf

This striking pendant looks great teamed up with warm beige and bright turquoise suede.

Linen Lariat

Materials:

2 metre (79in) stringing cord
6 x wrapped beads
12 x faux pearls

Tools:

Collapsible eye needle
Scissors

Instructions:

1 Make a knot in the stringing
thread within 10cm (4in) of the tail end.

2 Thread on one pearl, one wrapped and one
pearl bead. Make a second knot directly after the
last pearl added.

3 Leaving an 11cm (4³/₈in) gap, make another
knot, thread on a further pearl, a wrapped and a
pearl bead and make a second knot directly
after the last pearl added.

4 Continue in the same way until all
the beads are added.

5 To finish, knot the two ends
together to secure.

Creamy Blue Lariat

These pale blue pearls and creamy linen beads create a cool look for summer.

Precious Stone

Materials:

Pendant with central hole
2 x medium metal beads
1 metre (39½in) suede ribbon
2 x flat leather crimps
4 x crimp beads
Lobster clasp

Tools:

Round-nosed pliers
Flat-nosed pliers
Scissors

Instructions:

1 Place the two ends of
suede together and pass the loop
through the central hole of the
pendant. Pass the two ends of suede
through the loop and pull up, securing the suede on to
the pendant.

2 Thread on a crimp bead at the base of each length of
suede just above the pendant. Secure them using flat-
nosed pliers.

3 Thread a metal bead on to each length of suede and
add another crimp bead above each bead.

4 Finish by attaching the flat leather crimps and lobster
clasp after sizing the necklace to fit.

Polished Heart

This natural-looking necklace has knots instead of crimp beads around the copper-coloured beads.

Caribbean Colours

Materials:

A selection of large fashion beads
A selection of copper beads
Tiger tail wire
2 x calottes
2 x jump rings
1 x lobster clasp

Tools:

Cutting pliers
Round-nosed pliers

Instructions:

1 Lay the beads out either on a design board or a soft cloth and have a play at different variations and combinations of beads and colours.

2 When you are happy with the design, cut a length of tiger tail to the required length of necklace, allowing an extra 15cm (6in) each end for finishing.

3 Thread the beads on to the tiger tail in the required order.

4 Finish by adding the calottes, jump rings and lobster clasp in the usual manner.

14

Cool and Chunky

This shorter version of the necklace in turquoise and silver is a stunning alternative.

Cradled Heart

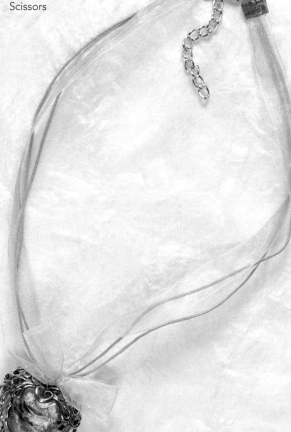

Materials:

Heart pendant
1 metre (39½in) organza ribbon
1 metre (39½in) stringing cord
2 x flat crimp end fasteners
2 x jump rings

Tools:

Flat-nosed pliers
Scissors

Instructions:

1 Cut organza ribbon and stringing cord to the required length for your necklace.

2 Thread both lengths through the pendant loop.

3 Place the cord and organza ends together, place in the crimp end fasteners and secure by squashing the metal plates together with flat-nosed pliers.

4 To add a final embellishment, thread a section of unused organza ribbon through the loop on the pendant, tie a bow and cut the ribbon ends at an angle.

Heart of Glass

*More delicate in colour, this version of the necklace
has white suede ribbon instead of cord.*

Glam Rocks

Materials:

1 metre (39½in) copper-coloured chain
7 x decorated feature beads
2 x jump rings
Lobster clasp

Tools:

Round-nosed pliers
Cutting pliers

Instructions:

1 Cut a section of copper chain to the required length of the necklace.

2 Thread on the seven large decorated beads.

3 Add the jump rings and lobster clasp to the ends of the chain.

Spring Fever

*These vibrant green beads make a striking necklace
with a spring-like feel.*

Caged Copper

Materials:

1 metre (39½in) wire mesh ribbon

A selection of copper beads

Large embellished bead

2 x flat leather crimps

2 x jump rings

Lobster clasp

Tools:

Flat-nosed pliers

Scissors

Instructions:

1 Thread the large embellished bead down to the centre point of the wire mesh ribbon and tie a double knot at each side of the bead to secure it.

2 Open up one end of the wire tube and slide a bead down until it sits next to the embellished bead. Tie a knot directly after the bead to close the wire mesh once again.

3 Next, pass a metal bead down over the mesh and tie a knot directly after it to secure it.

4 Continue to alternate in the same manner on either side of the large embellished bead until the necklace has reached the desired length.

5 Add the flat leather crimps, jump rings and lobster clasp to the ends to finish.

Note: Bear in mind when planning your design that knotting shortens the ribbon quite a bit.

Marvellous Mesh

Wire mesh ribbon is a fun and versatile material. In this pink and silver version of the necklace, some of it has been left beadless for a different effect.

Chain Reaction

Materials:

50cm (19¾in) large craft chain

15 x copper-coloured headpins

15 x copper-coloured jump rings

16 x crystals

1 x metre (39½in) ribbon

9 x copper-coloured beads

6 x shell slices

Tools:

Round-nosed pliers

Cutting pliers

Instructions:

1 Cut a length of chain to fit around the front section of the neck (the ribbon is the back section).

2 Wire the six shell slices with headpins, creating a loop at the top of each shell using round-nosed pliers.

3 Wire up the copper beads using headpins. Place a crystal at the bottom and sometimes at the top of the beads before creating the loop.

4 Use jump rings to attach the beads to the copper chain in your desired order.

5 Cut the ribbon in half, fold one piece together and pass the formed loop through the last link of the chain. Repeat on the other side. The ribbon is tied simply around the neck to secure.

Shellseekers

*These gorgeous pink and purple shell slices team up
perfectly with silver beads and mauve organza ribbon.*

Dot to Dot

Materials:

7 x embellished felt
beads

50cm (19¾in) nylon-
coated wire

2 x calottes

Jump ring

Lobster clasp

Suede ribbon

Tools:

Cutting pliers

Round-nosed pliers

Instructions:

1 Lay the nylon-
coated wire flat on a
table top and thread
on all seven felt beads.

2 When the necklace
has been correctly
sized, finish the ends
off in the usual way
using the calottes,
jump ring and
lobster clasp.

3 To embellish,
cut the suede into
lengths and tie a piece
between each bead,
cutting the ends to the
required length.

Beads and Bows

Silk ribbon replaces suede ribbon in this green and gorgeous version of the necklace.

Organza Garland

Materials:

1.5 metre (59¼in) organza ribbon

12 x crystals

12 x silver beads

Flat crimp end fasteners

Tools:

Flat-nosed pliers

Collapsible eye needle

Scissors

Instructions:

1 Cut the ribbon into three equal sections.

2 Take one piece of ribbon, thread it into the collapsible eye needle. Thread on one crystal and one silver bead, leaving a gap between each, and continue in this way until the fifth crystal bead has been added.

3 Take the second piece of ribbon and thread on four silver and four crystal beads alternately.

4 Using the final piece of ribbon, thread on four silver and three crystal beads alternately.

5 Place the three pieces of ribbon together so that they hang to three different lengths, then cut the ribbon ends. Place three ribbon ends together into the crimp end fastener and secure it using flat-nosed pliers. Repeat with the other three ribbon ends.

Ruby Crystals
*Ruby-coloured crystals and the palest of pink organza ribbon make a beautiful
necklace with a delicate and decadent style.*

Beach Lariat

Materials:

1 metre (39½in) stringing cord
14 x shell buttons

Tools:

Scissors

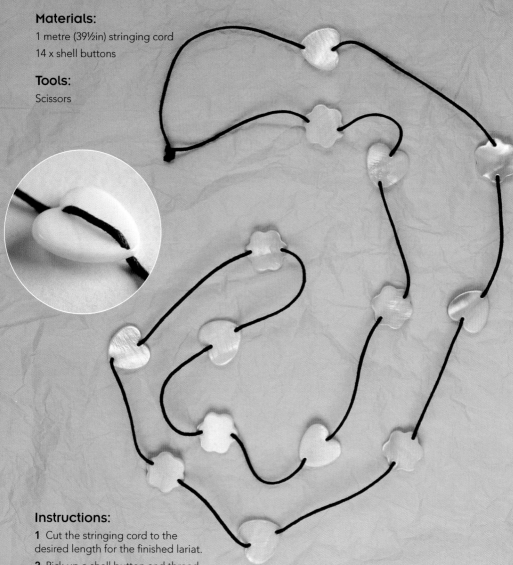

Instructions:

1 Cut the stringing cord to the
desired length for the finished lariat.

2 Pick up a shell button and thread
the cord through one of its holes, pass the button down to the tail end of the cord,
then thread the cord through the other hole.

3 Continue to thread buttons on to the cord, alternating hearts and flowers and
leaving a gap between each button.

4 When all the buttons are added, tie the two ends together with a knot to secure.

Hearts and Flowers

Green cord and yellow buttons give this longer lariat a natural, spring-like feel.
You need 2 metres (79in) of cord and twenty shell buttons for this version.

Faux Pearl Fancy

Materials:

1 metre (39½in) craft chain

31 faux pearls in various colours and sizes

31 x headpins

3 x jump rings

Lobster clasp

Tools:

Cutting pliers

Round-nosed pliers

Instructions:

1 Cut two lengths of chain, the first to come from the nape of the neck around to the front and the second to come from the nape of the neck around to the front, then to dangle down forming a 'Y' shape.

2 Create the 'Y' by linking the two chains together with a jump ring.

3 Size the necklace to fit. Remember you can cut excess length away at this point. Attach the lobster clasp to the ends of the chain using jump rings.

4 Wire the selection of faux pearls with headpins, creating a loop at the top of each pearl.

5 Before you start to add the pearls, check the length of the chain at the front, as it may need shortening.

6 Starting at the base, add pearls, continuing up the chain to finish.

Copper Tones

*Copper, bronze and gold-coloured faux pearls look amazing with
these deep-coloured crystals, making a necklace with a fiery feel.*

Roman Amulet

Materials:

Memory wire choker
10g size 8 seed beads
Pendant
2 metal feature beads

Tools:

Flat-nosed pliers

Instructions:

1 Using flat-nosed pliers, bend one end of the memory wire over to form a loop. This stops the beads from falling off the end.

2 Thread on the seed beads until you have not quite reached the centre of the choker.

3 Thread on the metal bead, then the pendant.

4 Repeat the bead sequence on the other side, leaving about 1cm (³/₈in) at the end for making the loop.

5 Once the beads are in position, bend the end into a loop to secure.

Cherry Red

*This version of the choker uses bright red size 6
seed beads and four silver-coloured feature beads,
which perfectly complement the gorgeous pendant.*

Petals Pendant

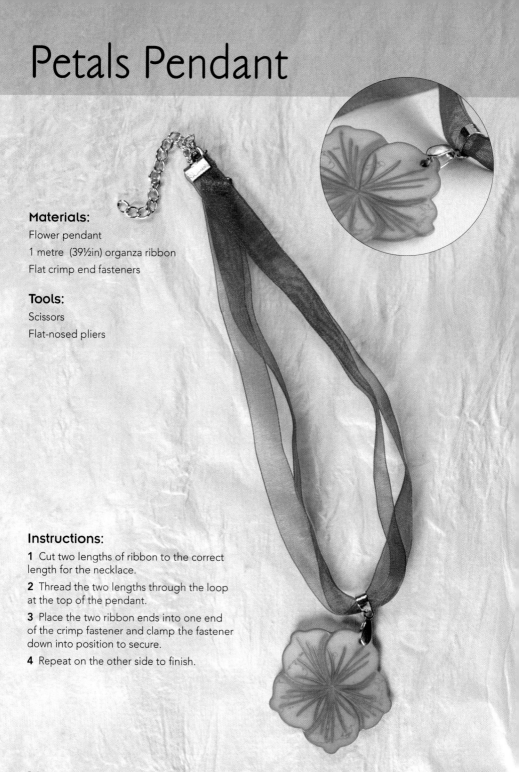

Materials:

Flower pendant

1 metre (39½in) organza ribbon

Flat crimp end fasteners

Tools:

Scissors

Flat-nosed pliers

Instructions:

1 Cut two lengths of ribbon to the correct length for the necklace.

2 Thread the two lengths through the loop at the top of the pendant.

3 Place the two ribbon ends into one end of the crimp fastener and clamp the fastener down into position to secure.

4 Repeat on the other side to finish.

Go Green

This pendant has a luscious look and when teamed up with the cool green ribbon it creates a pretty and sophisticated necklace.

Hidden Treasures

Materials:

1 metre (39½in) craft chain
10 x white glass beads
8 x blue glass beads
14 x blue size 6 seed beads
10 x silver size 6 seed beads
6 x bead cages
12 x headpins
20 x jump rings
Lobster clasp

Tools:

Cutting pliers
Round-nosed pliers

Instructions:

1 Cut two lengths of chain, the first to come from the nape of the neck around to the front, the second to come from the nape of the neck around to the front, then to dangle down forming a 'Y' shape.

2 Create the 'Y' shape by linking the two chains together with a jump ring.

3 Attach the lobster clasp once the necklace has been sized to fit (remember you can always cut any excess chain length away before attaching the clasp).

4 To make the 'caged' beads, take three blue and three white glass beads and push each one into a cage.

5 Wire the remaining twelve glass beads on to headpins, placing a contrasting seed bead at both ends of each glass bead. Form a loop at the top of each headpin above the beads.

6 Use jump rings to attach all the glass beads, caged and wired, to the chain, remembering to start at the base of the chain and work up.

Frosted Beauty
Subtle shades of pink and green and spiral cages in silver give this necklace a fresh, sparkling appeal.

Links in Time

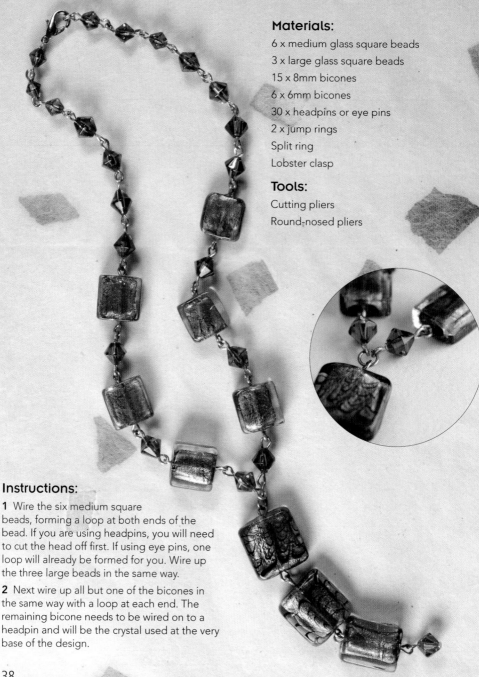

Materials:

6 x medium glass square beads
3 x large glass square beads
15 x 8mm bicones
6 x 6mm bicones
30 x headpins or eye pins
2 x jump rings
Split ring
Lobster clasp

Tools:

Cutting pliers
Round-nosed pliers

Instructions:

1 Wire the six medium square
beads, forming a loop at both ends of the
bead. If you are using headpins, you will need
to cut the head off first. If using eye pins, one
loop will already be formed for you. Wire up
the three large beads in the same way.

2 Next wire up all but one of the bicones in
the same way with a loop at each end. The
remaining bicone needs to be wired on to a
headpin and will be the crystal used at the very
base of the design.

3 Start by putting the bottom fringe together by reopening the loops of the large beads' wires and linking the beads together, remembering that the last bead needs to have the crystal on the headpin hanging from it.

4 Once the three large squares have been linked together, add two jump rings at the top. This allows the design to move.

5 Link the three medium squares with bicones alternately. Finish by adding four 8mm then three 6mm bicones (you can add more or fewer beads to alter the length of the necklace to fit).

6 Finally, add the lobster clasp and the split ring to the lasts links on the necklace.

Rosy Glow

The feature beads in this green and silver alternative
have the look of little pink roses captured in glass.

Vienna Delight

Materials:

1 metre (39½in) organza ribbon
1 x large feature bead
4 x medium feature beads
2 x flat leather crimps
Lobster clasp
2 x jump rings
Lobster clasp

Tools:

Flat-nosed pliers
Round-nosed pliers
Collapsible eye needle
Scissors

Instructions:

1 Cut the organza ribbon in half and thread each ribbon end into the collapsible eye needle.

2 Pass the two pieces of ribbon through one of the medium feature beads, the large bead and finally a second medium bead.

3 Leave a longer length at one side of the three beads to fit around the neck.

4 Rethread the needle on to one of the shorter ends of ribbon and thread a medium bead on. Decide on the length of the dangle and tie a knot under the bead to secure it. Cut away any tail end.

5 Repeat in the same way for the second dangle leaving this slightly longer than the first.

6 Determine the length of the necklace and cut the ribbon to size. Add the flat leather crimps and lobster clasp.

7 Finally, tie a leftover section of ribbon round the necklace ribbon with a single knot and trim the ends to make a decorative 'bow' effect. Repeat to make a second 'bow' on the other side of the necklace.

Black is Beautiful

The black and silver crackle-effect feature bead makes this version of the necklace dark and delicious.

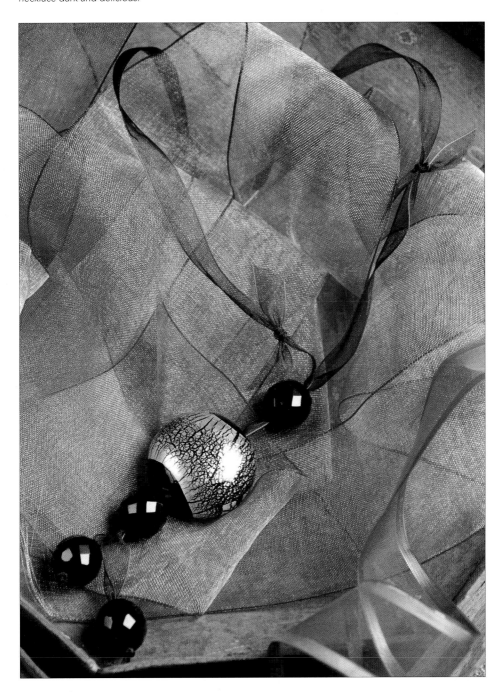

Celtic Creation

Materials:

Copper metal ornament
Stick-on jewels
50cm (19¾in) faux suede in two colours
Flat leather crimps
3 x jump rings
Lobster clasp
Jewellery glue

Tools:

Flat-nosed pliers
Scissors

Instructions:

1 Using the jewellery glue stick the jewels into position on the metal ornament. Allow to dry.

2 Cut the two pieces of faux suede to the correct length for the necklace. Feed them through the loop of the ornament.

3 Use the flat-nosed pliers to secure the flat leather crimps to the ends of the suede.

4 Finally attach the jump rings and lobster clasp.

Copper Sparkle

You can have great fun decorating these ornaments with your own choice of jewels. This ornament has a smaller central space so you end up with a more subtle effect.

African Queen

Materials:
Selection of large wooden and glass beads
1 metre (39½in) cotton stringing cord
Faux horn clasp
Jewellery glue

Tools:
Scissors

Instructions:

1 Thread the wooden and glass beads on to the cotton stringing cord in the desired order.

2 Pass the cord through the fixing hole on one side of the faux horn clasp.

3 Make a double knot and apply a small amount of glue to the knot to secure it.

4 Pass the other side of the cord through the second half of the clasp, pulling up as you go to pull the necklace together. Secure as before with a double knot and a small amount of glue to finish.

Knock on Wood

Big, bold, beautiful beads and a faux horn clasp give this wooden necklace an ethnic feel.

Publisher's Note

If you would like more books on the techniques shown,
try the following:
Beading Basics by Stephanie Burnham,
Barron's Educational Series, 2006
The Encyclopedia of Beading Techniques by
Sara Withers & Stephanie Burnham, Search Press, 2005
Designs for Beaded Jewellery Using Glass Beads and
Designs for Beaded Jewellery Using Natural Materials
both by Maria Di Spirito, Search Press, 2006

Acknowledgements

Many thanks to The Bead Scene for supplying all
the beads and equipment used in this book.

The Bead Scene
PO Box 6351
Towcester
Northamptonshire
NN12 7YX

Website: www.thebeadscene.com
email: Stephanie@thebeadscene.com
Tel: 01327 353639